© Copyright - All rights reserved.

You may not reproduce, duplicate or send the contents of this book without direct written permission from the author. You cannot hereby despite any circumstance blame the publisher or hold him or her to legal responsibility for any reparation, compensations, or monetary forfeiture owing to the information included herein, either in a direct or an indirect way.

Legal Notice: This book has copyright protection. You can use the book for personal purpose. You should not sell, use, alter, distribute, quote, take excerpts or paraphrase in part or whole the material contained in this book without obtaining the permission of the author first.

Disclaimer Notice: You must take note that the information in this document is for casual reading and entertainment purposes only.
We have made every attempt to provide accurate, up to date and reliable information. We do not express or imply guarantees of any kind. The persons who read admit that the writer is not occupied in giving legal, financial, medical or other advice. We put this book content by sourcing various places.

Please consult a licensed professional before you try any techniques shown in this book. By going through this document, the book lover comes to an agreement that under no situation is the author accountable for any forfeiture, direct or indirect, which they may incur because of the use of material contained in this document, including, but not limited to, — errors, omissions, or inaccuracies.

Copyrighted material

THIS BOOK BELONGS TO

TABLE OF CONTENTS

	No.
INTRODUCTION- Did You Know? (All About Anger)	9-15
Let's get to know you!	16-17
Why do I feel angry?	18
What things make me feel angry?	19
What are the things I am saying when I feel angry?	20
What does anger look like?	21
The circuit of anger.	22-23
5 anger rules.	24
My anger story.	25-26
Anger thermometer.	27
Anger and my body.	28

TABLE OF CONTENTS

	No.
Changing thoughts.	29-30
Relaxing page.	31
10 calm down tools.	32
What are my ways to calm down?	33-34
I say that or I don't say that.	35-36
Anger can be good or bad.	37-38
Anger management.	39
Anger pyramid.	40-41
Angry face- happy face.	42
Emotions card.	43-44
Anger diary.	45-59
5 quick tips and tricks.	60
Use my imagination.	61

TABLE OF CONTENTS

	No.
The stages of anger.	62
Understanding my anger.	63-64
Words connected to ANGER.	65
10 anger control affirmations.	66
Relaxing page.	67
Storm behaviors.	68-69
My anger triggers.	70
I'm talking to an adult about my anger.	71-73
I give a name to my anger.	74
Can I imagine myself angry?	75
My anger affects not only me but those around me.	76
How do I see the anger of those around me?	77-79

TABLE OF CONTENTS

	No.
This is what I learned about anger.	80-82
Positive thoughts.	83
Maze.	84
Best way to say I'm sorry.	85-86
Free Yourself!!!	87-88
Coloring pages.	89-94
DIPLOMA	

DID YOU KNOW?

This book is for children who are trying to get to know themselves better, to know their weaknesses, and who want to become a better version of themselves. In everyday life, we face a series of situations that infuriate us, but it is in our power to learn to control them. So, this is the goal of this book to help you, as a child, express your anger in the correct way. You must learn that anger is healthy, it helps you free yourself by expressing your feelings. But you must choose the right path so that it does not affect you or those around you.

DID YOU KNOW?

This book is more than a workbook! This book is a complex one in which you will find all the information about what anger means. This book includes tips and tricks to control anger, exercises, educational games, personal development, concrete images, questions and answers on your understanding, a personalized diary, a puzzle game, coloring pages to express feelings, a diploma, very useful in the process of knowing and accepting anger. Only by learning, knowing, and feeling this emotion, you will know how to act and react properly.

DID YOU KNOW?

This book is created for you! This book is created to understand your behavior and learn to control your anger. Through the activities included in the book you will rediscover yourself, you will know your limits, you will learn healthy habits and you will learn to make the right choices in those moments of anger. For a start, it is important to know a few essential things about what anger means and how it can affect you!

Have fun reading and get to work!

DID YOU KNOW?

- ✓ Anger is a basic and normal emotion like others- upset, joy, disappointment.

- ✓ It is normal to become angry in certain situations.

- ✓ When you feel angry is important to know how you could control it.

- ✓ It is important never to lose control.

- ✓ It is important to be calm, never break things, never hurt yourself or others.

- ✓ Mindfulness always helps you to stay in control.

DID YOU KNOW?

- ✓ Try to solve the problem without being angry.
- ✓ Control your anger if you don't want her to control you!
- ✓ Uncontrolled anger could affect your life and relationships.
- ✓ In some situations, your anger can have very serious consequences.
- ✓ It is necessary to know your limits and your triggers.
- ✓ Understanding the trigger for your anger helps you manage your reactions and your actions.

DID YOU KNOW?

- ✓ You must learn day by day how to express your anger in the correct way.

- ✓ Anger could be good or bad.

- ✓ Soothing tips and tricks can be very helpful in your moments of **anger**.

- ✓ In many cases behind anger are other hidden feelings and emotions.

- ✓ Anger can increase from irritation to anger and intense anger.

- ✓ An anger diary helps you analyze each situation and helps you see which strategy worked best for you.

DID YOU KNOW?

- ✓ You have to learn to behave differently in different situations of anger.
- ✓ Anger should not be used in a bad and destructive way.
- ✓ The feeling of anger consumes your energy.
- ✓ The feeling of anger does not mean the same thing as aggressive behavior.
- ✓ It is important to apologize if you made a mistake or something wrong.
- ✓ This book helps you to learn about your own anger and learn to accept that it exists.

Let's get to know you!

- Hello!
- I'm a
- I'm .... years old.
- I'm living with my ....
- Every day I'm learning that

it's okay to feel your feelings

Let's get to know you!

If you want, you can add other details, please write them down.

Every day I'm learning that

It's Okay to not be okay

Why do I feel angry?

Can you think why sometimes do you feel angry?
Please write down some examples.

EX: I feel angry when I lose at a swimming competition.

What things make me feel angry?

Please write down some examples.

EX: injustice, lies

What are the things I am saying when I feel angry?

EX: "Leave me alone!"

What does anger look like?

Imagine your anger. Can you sketch a picture of what it looks like when it comes to change your mood?

The circuit of anger.
22

Watch carefully and understand the whole circuit of anger!
Go to the next page and complete the tasks.

EX: I got a bad grade. I thought my parents would be disappointed in me. I started crying, so I unloaded. I calmed down.

The circuit of anger.

23

Learn the circuit of anger by filling the blanks with practical examples.

Something happened
1. _____
2. _____
3. _____
4. _____
5. _____

Thoughts appear
1. _____
2. _____
3. _____
4. _____
5. _____

I react
1. _____
2. _____
3. _____
4. _____
5. _____

I'm calming down
1. _____
2. _____
3. _____
4. _____
5. _____

5 anger rules.

It is okay to feel angry, but I must not forget a few rules:

1 I don't have to hurt anyone!

2 I don't have to hurt myself!

3 I don't have to destroy things!

4 I'm looking for a way to calm down as soon as possible!

5 I will ask an adult for help!

My anger story.

Remember and describe below your last anger episode.

What happened that made me feel angry?

_____
_____
_____
_____

How did my face looked in that moment of anger?

What kind of thoughts was going through my mind?

_____
_____
_____

Other feelings that tried me:

☑ sadness	☑ annoyed	☑ guilty
☑	☑	☑

What was my reaction?

☑ crying	☑ screaming	☑ hitting
☑	☑	☑

My anger story.

Remember and describe below your last anger episode.

What happened in the end?

_____
_____
_____

What were the consequences?

_____
_____
_____

Have I learned something about my anger?

_____
_____
_____

Were my deeds good?

(YES) OR (NO)

What would I do differently next time in the same situation?

_____
_____
_____
_____

Anger thermometer.

The anger grows and grows till becomes something really huge.

1

Show on the thermometer how are you feeling at this moment.

2

Write down which are your feelings now.

Anger and my body.

28

How does my body feel when I am angry?

My eyes feel ....

My ears feel ....

My mouth feels ....

My palms feel ....

My heart beats ....

My tummy feels ....

My feet feel ....

Other symptoms that you experience: ....

Changing thoughts.

Write down a few negative thoughts about a situation. Then, turn these negative expressions into positive ones.

Changing thoughts.

Write down a few negative thoughts about a situation. Then, turn these negative expressions into positive ones.

Relaxing page.

Take a moment to relax and color these pictures. Change your feelings.

10 calm down tools.

1. Count to 10.
2. Breath deeply and slowly.
3. Drink water.
4. Close your eyes and think to a place where you feel calm.
5. Use mindfulness to help.
6. Do your favorite activity: painting, drawing, reading, playing, listening to music.
7. Talk to someone about your feelings.
8. Ask for a hug.
9. Think of something happy.
10. Do some stretches.

What are my ways to calm down?

Circle the ways which are useful for you to calm down. Does it always work? Go to the next page and complete the tasks.

What are my ways to calm down?

Way to calm down	Does it always work? ✓ ✗		Write an example of how this worked?	How did I feel after?
EX: I'm drawing or painting.	✓		On days when I have a lot of homework, I get angry.	Relaxed and hardworking.
I'm talking to my best friend.				
I breath deeply and slowly.				
I'm taking a walk.				
I count to 10.				
I'm listening to music.				
I'm doing a puzzle.				
I'm writing about the problem.				
Write here other ways: →				

I say that or I don't say that. 35

When we are angry we often say less pleasant things. Write below, the words you would like to hear and those you would not want to hear when you are angry.

YES!
EX: I understand your anger. I'm with you.

NO!
EX: Did I tell you you shouldn't make it?

I say that or I don't say that.

When we are angry we often say less pleasant things. Write below, the words you would like to hear and those you would not want to hear when you are angry.

Anger can be good or bad.

Look carefully and understand why anger can be good or bad. Go to the next page and complete the tasks with practical examples.

ANGER IS GOOD

- ✓ you are able to express and communicate your emotions and your feelings
- ✓ you have the courage to take charge of the situation
- ✓ it helps you free yourself

ANGER IS BAD

- ✓ your thoughts are dark
- ✓ anger spoils your mood
- ✓ you can become aggressive

Anger can be good or bad.

Write down the situations in which you appreciated the anger as good or bad?

ANGER IS GOOD	**ANGER IS BAD**
EX: The thought that I could finish in 2nd place made me so angry that I increased my running pace and won.	**EX:** In a moment of anger, I destroyed my grandmother's favorite flowers.

Anger management.

Choose what is helpful when trying to manage anger. Put in the second jar things that are helpful for you.

- relax
- kick
- cry
- ask for help
- find a calming place
- scream
- threaten
- destroy things
- get hurt myself
- count to 10
- breath deeply and slowly
- drink water
- talk it out
- think positive
- blame others
- hit

Anger pyramid.

Do you know that in many cases behind anger are other hidden emotions? What emotions did you feel the last time you got angry? Circle these emotions. Go to the next page and complete the tasks.

ANGRY could mean

- sad
- guilt
- scared
- lonely
- unsure
- rejected
- shame
- nervous
- frustrated
- anxious
- offended
- trapped
- worried
- stressed
- disappointed
- uncomfortable
- jealous
- alone
- embarrassed
- tricked
- tired
- annoyed

Anger pyramid.

Complete the pyramid with other examples of what you think anger means.

Angry face- happy face.

Draw an angry face. After that, help the angry face to become happy.

ANGRY FACE

HAPPY FACE

Emotions card.

43

Below are several emotions. Circle the feelings that represent you generally. Explain them on the next page.

Emotions card.

44

Complete the tasks with examples.

EX: Generally, I am a happy person. I am very happy when I go on a trip with my parents.

_____
_____

_____
_____

_____
_____

_____
_____

_____
_____

_____
_____

_____
_____

Anger diary.

To be able to control the anger it is necessary to recognize when and why you feel angry. This anger diary is the perfect way to understand all the stages of anger (anger triggers, your response to anger). Please, record down a few of the serious moments of your anger and analyze each situation separately. Free yourself!!!

What happened that made me feel angry?	How did I feel? What did I think?	What was my reaction?	What were the consequences?
EX. I received a lot of homework for the next day.	I felt very sad. My teacher doesn't know that I'm invited to a party today.	I started crying.	I was upset and could not fully enjoy the party I was invited to.
1.			
2.			

Anger diary.

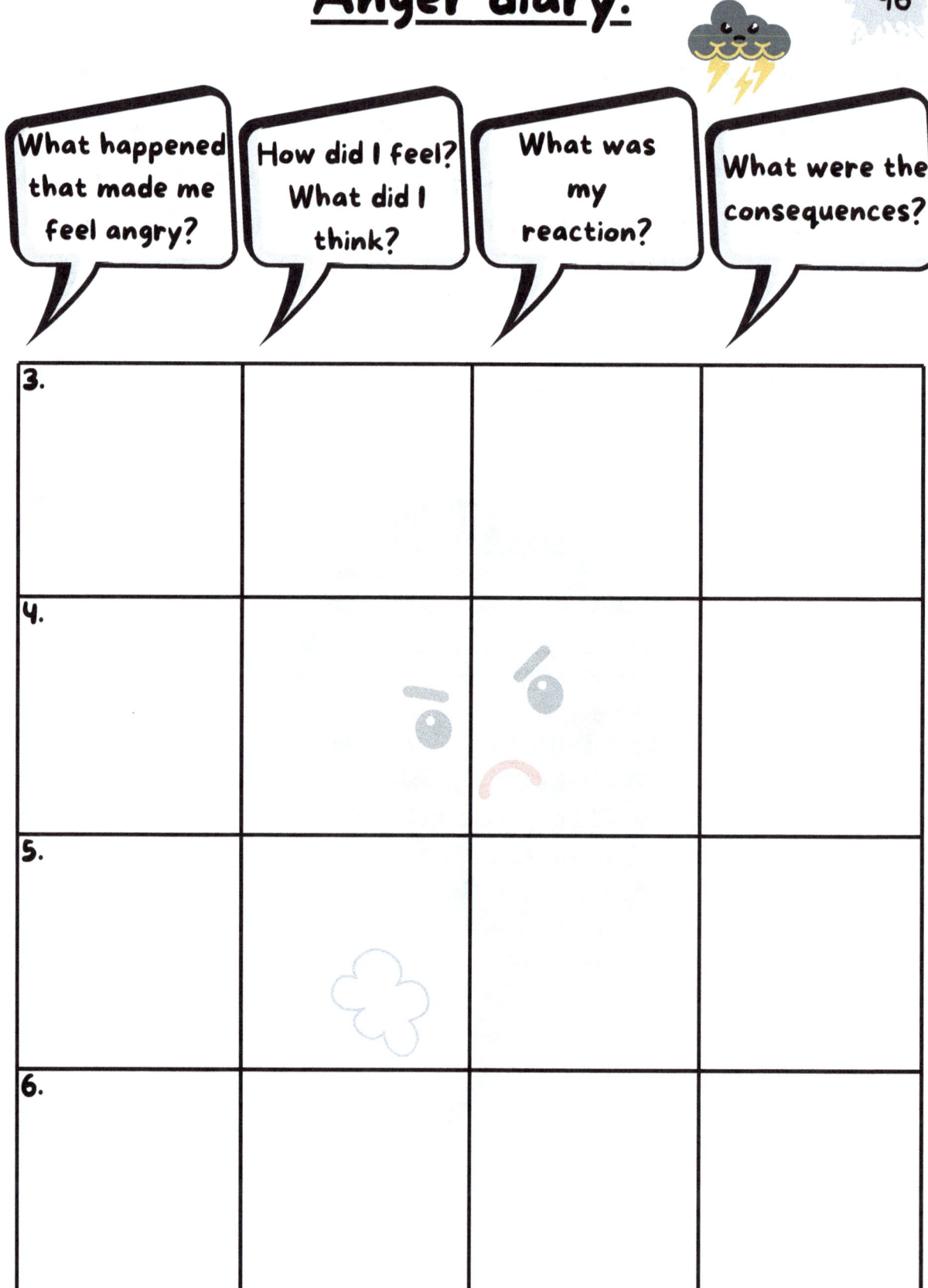

Anger diary.

What happened that made me feel angry?	How did I feel? What did I think?	What was my reaction?	What were the consequences?
7.			
8.			
9.			
10.			

Anger diary.

What happened that made me feel angry?	How did I feel? What did I think?	What was my reaction?	What were the consequences?
11.			
12.			
13.			
14.			

Anger diary.

What happened that made me feel angry?	How did I feel? What did I think?	What was my reaction?	What were the consequences?
15.			
16.			
17.			
18.			

Anger diary.

What happened that made me feel angry?	How did I feel? What did I think?	What was my reaction?	What were the consequences?
19.			
20.			
21.			
22.			

Anger diary.

51

What happened that made me feel angry?	How did I feel? What did I think?	What was my reaction?	What were the consequences?
23.			
24.			
25.			
26.			

Anger diary.

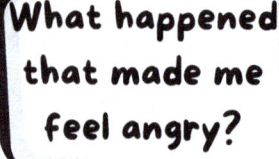

What happened that made me feel angry?	How did I feel? What did I think?	What was my reaction?	What were the consequences?
27.			
28.			
29.			
30.			

Anger diary.

53

After completing the diary, answer the following questions regarding the situations from 1 - 10.

- Am I proud of my deeds?
- Have I learned something about my anger?

✓ YES   ✗ NO

1.			
2.			
3.			
4.			
5.			
6.			
7.			
8.			
9.			
10.			

Copyrighted material

Anger diary.

54

After completing the diary, answer the following questions regarding the situations from 11 - 20.

- Am I proud of my deeds?
- Have I learned something about my anger?

✓ YES   ✗ NO

11.		
12.		
13.		
14.		
15.		
16.		
17.		
18.		
19.		
20.		

Anger diary.

55

After completing the diary, answer the following questions regarding the situations from 21 - 30.

	✓ YES	✗ NO	
21.			
22.			
23.			
24.			
25.			
26.			
27.			
28.			
29.			
30.			

Copyrighted material

Anger diary.

If you want to add something important to the anger diary, here are some rows.

Anger diary.

If you want to add something important to the anger diary, here are some rows.

Anger diary.

If you want to add something important to the anger diary, here are some rows.

_____
_____
_____
_____
_____
_____
_____
_____
_____
_____
_____
_____
_____
_____
_____
_____
_____
_____
_____
_____

Anger diary.

If you want to add something important to the anger diary, here are some rows.

5 quick tips and tricks.

When you are angry:

1. Never respond and react immediately.
2. Take time to calm down.
3. Stay positive.
4. Choose the right reaction and the right decision.

Don't forget!

5. All the less pleasant things and experiences go away, as does the anger.

TIPS & TRICKS

Do you practice these? Does it work?

_____
_____
_____
_____

Below is an angry boy. Use your imagination and write a short story about his anger.

_____
_____
_____
_____
_____
_____
_____
_____
_____
_____

The stages of anger. 62

Anger can have several stages. Break down your anger and respond to a few questions about your stages of anger.

Understanding my anger.

63

Understand your anger to find the most efficient and fastest way to calm down! Answer the questions below.

What do I think, am I angrier than others?

YES OR **NO**
_____
_____
_____
_____
_____

How fast do I get angry?
_____
_____
_____

How fast does my anger pass?
_____
_____
_____

How long does my anger last?
_____
_____
_____

Understanding my anger.

64

Understand your anger to find the most efficient and fastest way to calm down! Answer the questions below.

Does an episode of anger make me feel bad all day?

YES or NO _____

_____
_____
_____
_____

Does my anger affects relationships with others?

_____
_____
_____

What kind of method to calm down works for me?

_____
_____
_____

I learned that anger is normal but...

_____
_____
_____

Words connected to ANGER.

Discover in this puzzle the words that are connected with anger and anger management. Color them according to the shades in which the words at the bottom of the puzzle are written.

```
R I Y B T E N S I O N
E S W Q I B R E A T H
L U Q N A N X I O U S
A Z A N N O Y E D P T
X A Q F U R I O U S U
R T I N F L A M E D N
G C X C O N T R O L F
S A J S C R E A M V A
L L A V U J A S D H I
X M Z W C O U N T P R
```

SCREAM   RELAX   ANNOYED
CALM   INFLAMED   BREATH
TENSION   ANXIOUS   CONTROL
UNFAIR   COUNT   FURIOUS

10 anger control affirmations.

Use these statements in your daily routine. They will definitely help you!

1. I manage my behavior.
2. I manage my thoughts.
3. I am relaxed and calm.
4. I manage my own destiny.
5. I don't hurt anyone or me.
6. I find it easier to stay calm.
7. I am in full control.
8. I feel anger, but I can control it.
9. It is normal to feel angry from time to time.
10. Anger is just a feeling like any other.

Relaxing page.

Take a moment to relax and color these pictures. Change your feelings.

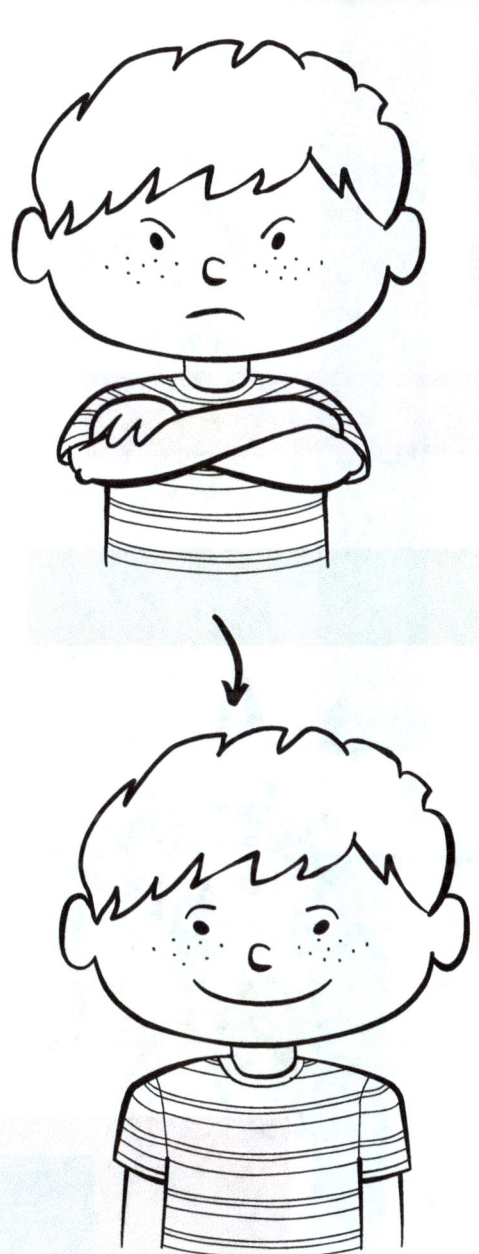

Storm behaviors.

When you were upset, did you experience these types of behaviors? Circle the ones you have experienced. Go to the next page and complete the tasks.

Storm behaviors.

69

Fill in the blanks with other types of behavior that you have experienced. Were they useful to you?

Explain below how they used you.

_____
_____
_____
_____
_____
_____
_____
_____

My anger triggers.

What triggered you? Underline with colors the potential triggers below.

Being ignored or excluded

Unable to finish tasks

Being misunderstood

Not understanding something at school

Disappointment

Unfair treatment

Being hungry or thirsty

Being powerless

Feeling unloved

Feeling frustrated

Too much homeworks

Feeling controlled

Being interrupted

Making a mistake

Getting hurt

Losing a game

Being late

Conflicts

Loud noises

Waiting

I'm talking to an adult about my anger.

Read each question or statement carefully. Go to the next pages and write the answer for each one. All of this will help you understand your anger!

1 Is anger good or bad? Give some examples.

2 Is it healthy to let anger control your mind and your body?

3 Sometimes anger can destroy. Give some examples.

4 What helps you control your anger?

5 Have you ever regretted a moment of anger? Could you tell?

6 Anger has consequences. Explain it.

7 Why is it important to apologize if you made a mistake?

8 Anger is a normal emotion, but ...

I'm talking to an adult about my anger.

Write down your answers from 1 to 4.

EX:
1 I think anger is good because when I'm angry I have the courage to say what bothers me. When my colleague took my homework without asking my permission, I was very angry, but I had the courage to take action and tell the teacher.

2

3

4

I'm talking to an adult about my anger.

Write down your answers from 5 to 8.

5 _____
_____
_____
_____

6 _____
_____
_____
_____

7 _____
_____
_____
_____

8 _____
_____
_____
_____

I give a name to my anger.

Make a list of possible names for your anger.

LIST OF NAMES:

_____	_____
_____	_____
_____	_____
_____	_____
_____	_____
_____	_____

Which of these do you think is the most appropriate?
Write it down with uppercases.

That's funny?

Can I imagine myself angry? 75

Take a look at the funny images below.
Which of these do you look like? Circle it.

That's funny?

YES! NO!

My anger affects not only me but those around me.

Complete below how do you think anger affects you or the people around you.

1 Myself

2 My parents

3 My friends

How do I see the anger of those around me?

Not only do we become angry, but so do those around us! Can you answer the questions below?

How do I feel when someone is angry at me?

_____
_____
_____
_____
_____
_____

How do I feel when someone around me loses his temper?

_____
_____
_____
_____

How do I feel when an angry person yells at me and could become aggressive?

_____
_____
_____
_____

How do I see the anger of those around me?

Not only do we become angry, but so do those around us! Can you answer the questions below?

What am I doing to calm my angry friend?

_____
_____
_____
_____

When someone is angry at me, do I become angry too?

_____
_____
_____
_____

How do I react to the anger of those around me?

_____
_____
_____
_____
_____
_____

How do I see the anger of those around me?

Answer the questions below.

How does the anger of those around me affect me?

_____
_____
_____
_____
_____
_____

If you want, you can sketch an episode in which someone around you was angry.

This is what I learned about anger

Write down what you learned about anger.

_____
_____
_____
_____
_____
_____
_____
_____
_____
_____
_____
_____
_____
_____
_____
_____
_____
_____
_____

This is what I learned about anger

Write down what you learned about anger.

_____
_____
_____
_____
_____
_____
_____
_____
_____
_____
_____
_____
_____
_____
_____
_____
_____
_____
_____
_____

This is what I learned about anger

Write down what you learned about anger.

_____
_____
_____
_____
_____
_____
_____
_____
_____
_____
_____
_____
_____
_____
_____
_____
_____
_____
_____
_____
_____
_____
_____

Positive thoughts.

Motivational thoughts help us when we are angry. Can you write below those thoughts that work in your case?

EX: Don't lose Focus   Believe in Yourself   Never give up

Maze.

Find the way to calm down.

Best way to say I'm sorry.

It is important to apologize if you made a mistake or something wrong. Here are the important steps to apologize. Go to the next page and complete the tasks.

1

I'm really sorry for .....

2

It was wrong because .....

3

Next time I will .....

4

Will you forgive me?

or

Do you think you can forgive me?

or

Can you forgive me, please?

Best way to say I'm sorry.   86

How do you apologize? Fill in the blanks.

EX: I'm really sorry for not being careful and losing your pet. It was wrong because I should have kept it on a leash permanently. Next time, I will be much more careful. Will you forgive me?

1 I'm really sorry for

2 It was wrong because

3 Next time I will

4 Will you forgive me?

Free Yourself!!!

If you are angry, free yourself! Draw or write what comes to your mind, if you want, you can scribble or even break this page. Do you feel better?

If you have not broken the page, it means that this book has reached its goal, namely to teach you to manage and release your anger. If you broke the page, it doesn't matter. The process of controlling anger is a long one, so continue.

Free yourself !!!

Color it!
Relax and put your anger aside!

Test your color here:

Color it!
Relax and put your anger aside!

Test your color here:

Color it!
Relax and put your anger aside!

Test your color here:

Color it!
Relax and put your anger aside!

Test your color here:

Color it!
Relax and put your anger aside!

Test your color here:

Color it!
Relax and put your anger aside!

Test your color here:

DIPLOMA

THIS CERTIFICATE IS PRESENTED TO

_____

FOR LEARNING ABOUT ANGER MANAGEMENT AND COMPLETING ALL THE ACTIVITIES IN THE BOOK.

DATE:

THANK YOU!

WE HOPE YOU ENJOYED OUR BOOK!

As a small family company, we want to deliver only the best content and your experience is very important for us!

www.ingramcontent.com/pod-product-compliance
Lightning Source LLC
LaVergne TN
LVHW060335080526
838202LV00053B/4479